Wildflowers and Trees of West Virginia

Wildflowers and Trees of West Virginia
Identifying the State's Flora, Including Shrubs and Vines

Christopher M. Gatens & Emily Grafton
Illustrations by Erin Turner

Charleston, West Virginia

© 2009 Christopher M. Gatens, Emily Grafton, and Erin Turner

All rights reserved. No part of this book may be reproduced in any form
or means, electronic or mechanical, including photocopying, recording,
or by any information storage and retrieval system,
without permission in writing from the publisher.

Library of Congress Catalog Number 2009930747

ISBN-13: 978-1-891852-63-3
ISBN-10: 1-891852-63-9

Printed in China
First Edition

10 9 8 7 6 5 4 3 2 1

Book and cover design: Mark S. Phillips

Distributed by:

West Virginia Book Company
1125 Central Ave.
Charleston, WV 25302
www.wvbookco.com

Table of Contents

Introduction vii

Yellow Wildflowers 1

Orange Wildflowers. 24

Red Wildflowers. 29

Purple Wildflowers 34

Blue Wildflowers 38

Pink Wildflowers 59

White Wildflowers. 77

Shrubs and Vines 108

Trees 136

Index. 180

Introduction

West Virginia's wide range of plant diversity allows the state to be a true "garden of earthly delights" for the tree and wildflower enthusiast. The state's native plant diversity owes to the fact that it resides in a geographical region where northern and southern latitudes converge, providing many different growing seasons, seasonal temperature and rainfall ranges, and habitats. When considering all of the state's plant species, one will also note the non-native species introduced from Europe, Asia, and elsewhere. Many of these non-natives have naturalized to become a part of our state flora, like it or not.

This field guide, *Wildflowers and Trees of West Virginia: Identifying the State's Flora, Including Shrubs and Vines* can be an invaluable tool for the identification of common trees and wild-growing flowers in West Virginia. Common wildflowers—found in woods, hollows, and fields—have been arranged herein by the color of their flower structure. A brief plant description, its flowering season and habitat, and an illustration have been provided for each entry in the flower section.

The woody vegetation in the guide has been grouped into three categories: trees, shrubs, and woody vines. A brief description of the species includes such characteristics as bark color, plant height, habitat, and leaf structure. Illustrated drawings of leaves, needles, and/or fruit accompany each entry in this section, as well as a silhouette of most of the trees.

Use this guide as a helpful, easy-to-use interpretive aid, either while out hiking through the West Virginia landscape, or at home selecting native plants for your yard or garden. Either way, enjoy this book while you enjoy our beautiful state!

Yellow Wildflowers

Bellwort
Uvularia spp.
Spring. Plants are 6 inches to 2 feet tall. Forked stems with drooping-yellowish-bell-shaped flowers. Found in mature woods with rich soils.

Yellow Wildflowers

Birdsfoot Trefoil
Lotus corniculatus
Spring to fall. Plants have vines across the ground with yellow-snapdragon-like flowers. Invasive—sown for ground cover.

Yellow Wildflowers

Black-eyed Susan
Rudbeckia hirta
Summer. Plant grows 1 to 2.5 feet tall with a rough, hairy stem. The flowers heads measure 4-5 inches across and are yellow with a purplish-brown center. The plant is common in fields and along roadsides.

Yellow Wildflowers

Butter & Eggs
Linaria vulgaris
Spring to fall. Plants are 1 to 3 feet tall with numerous, hairy leaves. Flowers are hood-shaped with 2 lips. Plant thrives in sunny, disturbed soils.

Yellow Wildflowers

Canada Goldenrod
Solidago canadensis
Summer to fall. Plants are 2 inches to 7 feet tall with numerous toothed-smooth leaves. Flowers are plume-like at the top of the stem. Likes moist to dry openings and thickets.

Yellow Wildflowers

Colts Foot

Tusilago farfara

Spring. Plants grow up to 1.5 inches tall with basal leaves only, which appear after the flowers. Golden flower discs are 1 inch across. Plant likes dry, disturbed soils.

Yellow Wildflowers

Common Beggar-ticks
Bidens vulgata
Late summer to fall. Plants are 1 to 5 feet tall with purplish stems and 3-parted leaves. Flower heads are .5 to 1 inch wide. Grow in waste places, roadsides and thickets.

Yellow Wildflowers

Common Cinquefoil
Potentilla simplex
Spring to early summer. Plants are trailing, growing up to 8 inches tall. Five-parted leaves with toothed-edges. Flowers are .25 to .5 inches across. Plant likes dry soil, waste places.

Yellow Wildflowers

Common Mullein
Verbascum thapsus
Summer to fall. Plants are 3 to 6 feet tall with large fuzzy gray-green leaves. Yellow flowers are on terminal spikes. Appear along roadsides and other disturbed soils.

Yellow Wildflowers

Evening Primrose
Oenothera biennis
Summer to fall. Plants are two inches to 5 feet tall, with lance-shaped leaves. The yellow, lemon-scented flowers grow nearly 2 inches across, and bloom in late day. Plant likes dry fields and roadsides.

Yellow Wildflowers

Smooth Foxglove
Aureolaria laevigata
Summer to fall. Plants grow up to 5 feet tall with opposite, oblong to lance-shaped leaves. Flowers are .25 to .5 inches long; funnel-shaped with fluted edges. It grows in dry woods and thickets.

Yellow Wildflowers

Golden Alexander's
Zizia aptera
Spring to summer. Plants are 1 to 3 feet tall with round basal leaves and heart-shaped stem leaves. Flowers are less than .25 inch wide. Plant commonly found in woodlands.

Yellow Wildflowers

Lousewort
Pedicularis canadensis
Spring. Plants are 6 to 18 inches tall with a rosette of fern-like leaves. Snapdragon-like flowers occur in a terminal cluster. Grow in moist to dry woodlands.

Yellow Wildflowers

Moth Mullein

Verbascum blattaria
Summer to fall. Non-native. Plants are 2 to 4 feet tall with linear-triangular leaves clasping the stems. Cup-shaped, .5 inch flowers are white or yellow in a loose, terminal cluster. Grow in old fields and waste places.

Yellow Wildflowers

Pale Touch-me-not
Impatiens pallida
Summer to fall. Plants are 4 to 6 inches tall with widely spaced, egg-shaped leaves. Its dangling, tubular flowers are up to 1 inch long. Appears in open, wet places.

Yellow Wildflowers

Rattlesnake Weed

Hieracium venosum

Spring to summer. Basal flattened-rosette of purple-veined leaves. Its 8 to 15 inch stalk bears .5 to 1 inch flowers on branch tips. These plants appear in dry, open woods.

Yellow Wildflowers

Common St. Johnswort
Hypericum perforatum
Summer to fall. Plants are 1 to 1.5 feet tall with many elliptical leaves with translucent dots. Flowers are up to 1 inch across. Plant appears in fields and disturbed soils and along roadsides.

Yellow Wildflowers

Yellow Woodland Violet
Viola pubescens
Spring. Plants are 6 to 18 inches tall with 2 to 4 inch heart-shaped leaves along the main stem. Individual flowers are .5 to 1 inch at the top of stem. Likes rich woodlands.

Yellow Wildflowers

Thin Leaved Sunflower
Helianthus decapetalus
Summer to fall. Plants are 3 to 6 feet tall with opposite, rough and toothed lance-shaped leaves. Flowers are 3 to 5 inches across. These are common along roadsides.

Yellow Wildflowers

Trout Lily

Erythronium americanum
Spring. Plants are 4 to 8 inches tall. These two-leaved plants tend to grow in dense patches. The leaves are linear-shiny, mottled with brownish spots. Plants prefer bottomland soils.

Yellow Wildflowers

Woodland Sunflower

Helianthus divaricatus
Summer to fall. Plants are 3 to 6 feet tall with opposite, lance-shaped leaves that nearly clasp the stem. The 1.5 to 3 inch flowers are the earliest flowering sunflower. Prefers dry banks and forest edges.

Yellow Wildflowers

Wreath Goldenrod
Solidago caesia
Summer to fall. Plants are 1 to 3 feet tall with a round, bluish stem with alternate-arching narrow leaves. Flowers appear in a spiral-like pattern in leaf axils. Prefers a woodland habitat.

Yellow Wildflowers

Yellow Flag Iris

Iris pseudoacaris
Summer. Plant is 2 to 3 feet tall with slender, sword-like leaves. The 3 to 4 inch flowers have 3 irregular petals. This plant is highly invasive in its natural habitats— do not cultivate! Appears in marshes and along streams.

Orange Wildflowers

Butterfly Milkweed

Asclepias tuberosa

Summer. Plants are 1 to 3 feet tall and densely covered with narrow leaves. The 1 to 3 inch flowers appear in terminal clusters. A major butterfly magnet, it grows in fields and disturbed soils.

Orange Wildflowers

Day Lily
Hemerocalus fulva
Spring to summer. Plants are 2 to 4 feet tall with long linear leaves. Flowers are 3 to 5 inches long with 6-reflexed petals. Appear along roadsides, edges of trails, and in open fields.

Orange Wildflowers

Field Hawkweed
Hieracium caespitosum
Spring to fall. Plants are 10 to 18 inches tall with basal rosette of leaves. Terminal cluster of flower heads. Grows in fields and along roadsides.

Orange Wildflowers

Spotted Touch-me-not
Impatiens capensis
Summer to fall. Plants are 2 to 4 feet tall with egg-shaped leaves and a round stem. The stem juice soothes pain from poison ivy or nettles. The 1 inch, pendulous flowers are cone-shaped with fluted edges. Likes shady, moist ground.

Orange Wildflowers

Turk's Cap Lily
Lilium superbum
Summer. Plant is 4 to 5 feet tall. The lance-shaped leaves appear on stems in 3 to 8 inch whorls. The flowers are orange, showy, and the petals curved upward to resemble a turban. Most abundant in the higher elevations.

Red Wildflowers

Bee Balm
Monarda didyma
Summer. Plants are 1 to 3 feet tall. Flower heads are 2 to 3 inches wide with numerous arching tubular flowers having a minty fragrance. A butterfly magnet, these plants grow in moist thickets, open banks, and roadside ditches.

Red Wildflowers

Cardinal Flower
Lobelia cardinalis
Summer to fall. Plants are 2 to 5 feet tall with numerous smooth-toothed leaves. The flowers alternate in a spike at top of stem. Attracts hummingbirds and butterflies. Likes moist to dry openings and thickets.

Red Wildflowers

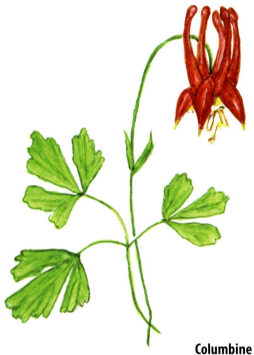

Columbine
Aquilegia canadensis
Spring. Plants are 1 to 2 feet tall. Its oval leaves have multiple lobes. The flowers are showy and resemble spurs that point upward. Likes woodlands and rocky slopes.

Red Wildflowers

Fire Pink
Silene virginica
Spring. Plants are 1 to 2 feet tall. Leaves are opposite and lance-shaped. Flower petals are deep crimson. Likes dry and open woodlands.

Wake Robin
Trillum erectum
Spring. Plants are 6 to 16 inches tall with 3 heart-shaped 3 to 8 inch long leaves in a single tier. Its single, dangling flower is up to 3 inches across and has 3 petals. This plant appears in moist, rich woodland soils.

Purple Wildflowers

Blue Cohosh
Caullophylum thalictroides
Spring. Plant is 1 to 3 feet tall with showy foliage that stays soft bluish-green all season. Flowers are less than .5 inch wide with purple-green to yellow-green sepals. Found in mature woods with rich soils.

Purple Wildflowers

Jack-in-the-Pulpit

Arisaema triphyllum

Spring. Plants are 1 to 3 feet tall with large 3-part leaves. The flowers are on a club-shaped structure enveloped in a purple-striped hood. This plant prefers the deep-rich soils of woodland hillsides.

Purple Wildflowers

Skunk Cabbage
Symplocarpus foetidus
Early spring. Plants are 1 to 2 feet tall. Its tiny flowers grow on a club-shaped structure. Large cabbage-like leaves melt the snow as they emerge in late winter. Likes low, swampy ground.

Purple Wildflowers

Wild Ginger
Asarum canadense
Spring. Low to the ground plant that commonly bears two soft heart-shaped leaves that measure 2 to 4 inches wide. The bell-shaped flower is purple. Plant is common in rich woods.

Blue Vervain
Verbena hastata
Summer to fall. Plant is 1.5 to 5 feet tall. Its main stem is coarse and 4-sided. Flower stalks are branched; flowers are less than 1/2 inch. Grows in open fields.

Blue Wildflowers

Blue-eyed Grass
Sisyrinchium angustifolium
Summer. A plant with thin, grass-like leaves measuring up to 1 foot tall. The small blue flowers have 5 petals and are less than 1 inch wide. Plant is found in fields.

Blue Wildflowers

Bluebells

Mertensia virginica

Spring. Plants are 1 to 1.5 feet tall with numerous nodding, 1 inch flowers enveloped in large, soft-green, elliptical leaves. Plant prefers deep rich soils found along streams and moist, rich, hillside coves.

Blue Wildflowers

Bluets
Houstonia spp.
Spring to fall. Plants are 2 to 7 inches tall with slender stems. Cross-shaped flowers occur in tufts on lawns, fields and trails.

Blue Wildflowers

Chickory
Chicorum intybus
Summer to fall. Plants are 1 to 5 feet tall with oblong leaves. The numerous ray-flowers with notched edges are 1 inch across. Common along roadsides.

Blue Wildflowers

Common Monkey Flower
Mimulus ringens
Summer to fall. Plants are 2 to 4 feet tall with opposite-linear leaves. Its lavender flowers have 2 lips. Plant is found at the edges of streams, ponds and lakes.

Blue Wildflowers

Wild Bergamot
Monarda fistulosa
Summer to fall. Plants are 2 to 4 feet tall. A square-stem bears opposite, tooth-edged oval to lance-shaped leaves. The 1 inch tubular flowers radiate from a compact head with a minty fragrance. Found in thickets and old fields.

Blue Wildflowers

Dwarf Crested Iris
Iris cristata
Spring. Plants grow 4 to 8 inches tall with flat, lance-shaped leaves. Plants have a single 2.5 to 3 inch violet blue, bearded flower. Likes moist soils and edge habitats.

Blue Wildflowers

Dwarf Larkspur

Delphinium tricorne

Spring. Plants range from 6 inches to 2 feet tall and have deeply dissected leaves. Its deep blue or purple flowers have curled sepals and petals in a spur-like shape. Grows in deep, moist-rich soils of woodland hillsides.

Blue Wildflowers

Great Lobelia
Lobelia siphilitica
Summer to fall. Plants are 2 to 4 feet tall with elliptical leaves that taper to a point. Its 1 inch tubular flowers are violet-blue with a lipped edge. Attracts butterflies. Prefers moist soils.

Blue Wildflowers

Ground Ivy
Glechoma hederacea
Spring to summer. Plants are creeping, with 2 to 8 inch stems with round-lobed leaves. Tubular flowers at only .25 inch appear in whorls around stem. Common in lawns, fields, and waste places.

Blue Wildflowers

Heal-all
Prunella vulgaris
Spring to fall. Plants are 4 to 10 inches tall with square stems and variably-shaped leaves. Its .5 inch, tubular flowers grow in a long spike. A butterfly magnet, heal-all grows in lawns and at waste places.

Blue Wildflowers

Mad-dog Skullcap

Scutellaria lateriflora

Summer to fall. Plants are 1 to 2 feet tall with opposite, rounded, slender leaves. Its pairs of tubular flowers appear in dense clusters; the flowers are .25 inch long. Likes moist habitats.

Blue Wildflowers

Mistflower

Eupatorium coelestinum
Summer to fall. Plants are 1 to 3 feet tall with opposite, crinkly-textured, triangular leaves. Numerous feathery flowers appear at the tops of stems. Likes moist woodlands and fields.

Blue Wildflowers

New England Aster
Symphyotrichum novae-angliae
Fall. Plants are 2 to 4 feet tall.
Alternate, lance-shaped leaves
claps the stems. Showy, up to one
inch wide blue to purple flowers
on many terminal branches. Likes
moist fields and roadsides.

Blue Wildflowers

Periwinkle
Vinca minor
Spring. Plant with opposite, dark, evergreen leaves growing on a trailing stem. The 1 to 1.5 inch flowers are blue. The plant is common throughout the state, and frequently used as a ground cover.

Blue Wildflowers

Spiderwort

Tradescantia spp.
Summer. Plant measures 1 to 2 feet tall with grass-like, 1 to 2 inch leaves. The flower is up to 3 inches across with 3 showy blue petals. Plant is found in woods, thickets and old fields.

Blue Wildflowers

Tall Bellflower
Campanula americana
Summer to fall. Plants are 2 to 4 feet tall with lance-shaped, toothed leaves, 3 to 6 inches long. Star-shaped, 1 inch wide flowers arise from leaf axils at top of the stem. Found in moist thickets and woodlands.

Blue Wildflowers

Vipers Bugloss
Echium vulgare
Summer to fall. One to 3 feet tall and covered with bristly hairs. Has densely packed 2 to 6 inch oblong leaves. Its showy, funnel-shaped flowers have protruding stamens. Flowers are bluish to lavender. Likes disturbed soils, especially roadsides.

Blue Wildflowers

Wild Blue Phlox
Phlox divaricata
Spring. Plants are 8 to 20 inches tall. Its paired, narrow leaves are up to 2 inches long and widely spaced. Flowers are tubular at the base and open to 5 spreading petals that are 1 inch across in a loose cluster. Prefers moist woodland soils.

Blue Wildflowers

Wild Geranium
Geranium maculatum
Spring. Plants are up to 2 feet tall with deeply divided showy leaves. The flowers are up to 1.5 inches wide, appearing in loose clusters at the top of the stem. Most common in open woodlands.

Pink Wildflowers

Beard Tongue
Penstemon spp.
Spring and summer. Plants are 1 to 2 feet tall with hairy stems and leaves. Tubular white to lavender flowers are 1 to 2 inches long. A bee magnet, this plant prefers dry roadbanks, trails, and open fields.

Pink Wildflowers

Bouncing Bet

Saponaria officinalis

Summer. Plants are 1 to 2 feet tall with opposite, smooth leaves. Its pink flowers are 1 inch wide with 5-notched petals. Plants grow in disturbed soils and at edges of roads and railroads.

Pink Wildflowers

Common Milkweed
Asclepias syriaca
Summer to fall. Plants 3 to 5 feet tall with large opposite leaves. Flowers are fragrant, violet, pendulous clusters. Major source of butterfly nectar. Commonly found in open fields, waste places and roadsides.

Pink Wildflowers

Creeping Phlox

Phlox stolonifera

Spring. Plants are 6 to 8 inches tall with opposite oblong leaves on creeping stems. Its pink flowers are 1 to 2 inches across. Prefers the moist rich soils of woodlands.

Pink Wildflowers

Crown Vetch
Coronilla varia

Summer. This trailing plant grows 1 to 2 feet long with multiple dissected oval leaflets. Its pink flowers have winged petals. Plant is an invasive ground cover found on roadsides and in other disturbed soils.

Pink Wildflowers

Dame's Rocket
Hesparis matrinalis
Spring to summer. Plants are 2 to 3 feet tall with large leaves. Its purple and pink flowers form dense spikes. Invasive, this plant is found in moist road banks, fields, and thickets.

Pink Wildflowers

Deptford Pink
Dianthus armeria
Spring to summer. Plants are 6 inches to 2 feet tall with a thin, hairy stem supporting several 5-petaled, .5 inch pink flowers. Found in lawns, dry fields, waste places and along trails.

Pink Wildflowers

Field Thistle
Cirsium vulgare
Summer to fall. Plants are 2 to 6 feet tall with spine-covered, lance-shaped leaves. Its pink flower tufts are 2 to 3 inches wide. Grow in waste places.

Pink Wildflowers

Fireweed

Epilobium angustifolium
Summer. The plants are 1 to 5 feet tall with many, narrow, lance-shaped leaves. The pink/red flowers appear in large terminal spikes. These plants grow along road banks and in waste places.

Pink Wildflowers

Hepatica
Hepatica spp
Spring. Plants are 4 to 6 inches tall with 3 round-lobed or sharp-lobed leaves. Dainty pink flowers have 5 to 9 showy petal-like sepals. Grow in moist, rich woods.

Pink Wildflowers

Ironweed
Vernonia noveboracensis
Summer to fall. Plants are 3 to 6 feet tall with large, coarse, lance-shaped leaves. The stem branches at the top and bears clusters of pinkish-red to purplish flowers. Prefers the moist soils of fields, stream banks and roadside ditches.

Pink Wildflowers

Joe Pye Weed

Eupatorium fistulosum
Summer to fall. Plants are 3 to 7 feet tall with a round, smooth stem. Leaves grow in tiered whorls. Pink fluffy flowers grow in rounded clusters at tops of stems. A butterfly magnet, it grows in the moist soils of fields, stream banks, and wet ditches.

Pink Wildflowers

Pasture Rose

Rosa caroliniana
Summer. One to 3 feet tall. The plants have straight thorns and widely spaced, coarsely-toothed, divided leaves. Have single, 2 inch wide beautiful pink flowers. Grow in dry woods and pastures.

Pink Wildflowers

Rose Pink

Sabatia angularis

Summer. Plants are 12 to 18 inches tall with a four-angled, winged stem. The leaves are opposite, without a stalk. The 1 inch flowers are pink or occasionally white, and loosely spaced on the branch tips. Found on roadsides and at openings.

Pink Wildflowers

Rose Polygala
Polygala sanguinicea
Summer to fall. Plants are 4 to 10 inches tall with linear leaves, 1 inch long. Its thimble-shaped flower heads are packed with tiny pink and white flowers. Prefers the moist soils of fields and other openings.

Pink Wildflowers

Swamp Rose Mallow

Hibiscus moscheutos

Summer. Plants are 4 to 7 feet tall with alternate, 4 to 7 inch long heart-shaped leaves. The 2 to 3 inches pink flowers appear at the tops of the stems in clusters. This plant grows in wetlands.

Pink Wildflowers

Trailing Arbutus
Epigaea repens
Early spring. Plants are flattened and trailing, growing up to 2 inches tall. Linear dull-green, leathery leaves are 1 to 4 inches. Its tubular pink flowers are .5 inch, occurring in miniature bouquets. Flowers emit a rich, spicy, sweet fragrance. Grows in sandy, rocky, acidic soils with partial shade.

Pink Wildflowers

Wild Bleeding Heart
Dicentra eximia
Spring to summer. Plants are 8 to 20 inches tall with large, soft, fern-like, bluish-green leaves. Its pink to deep magenta heart-shaped flowers, measuring .75 inch, dangle from an arching stem. Found among rocky banks and woodlands.

White Wildflowers

Black Cohosh
Cimcifuga racemosa
Summer. Plants grow up to 7 feet tall and have large, deeply-divided leaves. Its many small (up to .5 inch) white flowers are in tight clusters on candelabra-like branches. Prefers mature woods with rich soils.

White Wildflowers

Bloodroot
Sanguinaria canadensis
Spring. Plant grows up to 6 inches tall. One broad, palm-shaped bluish-green leaf cradles a 2 inch wide creamy-white flower. Grow in mature woods with rich soils.

White Wildflowers

Boneset
Eupatorium perfoliatum
Summer to fall. Plant stems are 2 to 6 feet tall with hairy, large, opposite leaves that clasp the stem. The clusters of small white colored flower heads measure .75 inches across. Grow in moist soils along streams and ditches.

Bugleweed

Lycopis virginicus
Summer to fall. One to 3 feet tall plants have clusters of tubular whitish flowers in tiers along the stem. It has sharply toothed leaves 3 to 4 inches long and 1 inch wide. Plant prefers moist thickets, and wet trail and road edges.

White Wildflowers

Canada Violet
Viola canadensis
Spring. Plant is 6 to 14 inches tall with a leafy stem. The flowers have 5 whitish petals with a purple-tinged underside. The leaves are heart-shaped and 2 inches. These grow in the moist, rich soils of woodlands.

White Wildflowers

Common Arrowhead or
Duck Potato

Saggitaria latifolia

Summer to fall. Plants are 1 to 4 feet tall with large arrow-shaped leaves. The white flowers have 3 showy petals and grow up to 1 inch across. Prefers aquatic areas, wet ditches and pond edges.

White Wildflowers

Common Chickweed
Stellaria media

Spring. The plants are up to 8 inches tall with a trailing stem. Small .5 inch leaves are oval shaped. The small, white flowers have cleft petals. Prefers lawns and disturbed sites.

White Wildflowers

Common Spring Beauty

Claytonia virginica

Spring. A low plant that bears opposite, lance-shaped leaves up to 4 inches long. The flowers are white to pink. Plant is found in rich woods throughout the state.

White Wildflowers

Cut-leaved Toothwort
Cardamine concapenata
Spring. Plants are 6 to 15 inches tall. Commonly, has two separate leaves that are strongly divided into 3-toothed segments. The white to pinkish flowers appear in terminal, dangling clusters. Prefer the rich soils of woodlands.

White Wildflowers

Daisy Fleabane

Erigeron annuus

Summer to fall. Plants are 1 to 5 feet with hairy leaves and stems. The flowers are small, ragged white ray flowers with yellow centers, growing up to .5 inch across. Grow along roadsides and waste places.

White Wildflowers

Dutchman's Breeches
Dicentra cucullaria
Spring. Plants are 4 to 12 inches tall with finely dissected leaves. Its drooping white flowers have fused petals. Plant prefers the deep, rich soils of woodland hillsides.

White Wildflowers

Foam Flower

Tiarella cordifollia

Spring. Compact plants at 6 to 12 inches have lobed, hairy leaves. Its numerous, small white flowers are only .25 wide each, feathery and showy. Grow in moist woodland soils.

White Wildflowers

Garlic Mustard
Alliaria petiolata
Spring. Plants are 1 to 3 feet tall with heart-shaped leaves. The flowers are .25 inch long, each with 4 showy, white petals. Highly invasive in natural habitats. Prefer stream banks, bottomland forests.

Great White Trillium
Trillium grandiflorum
Spring. Plants are 6 inches to nearly 2 feet tall, with 3 heart-shaped, tapering leaves. White flower petals turn pink as they mature. Prefer the moist, rich soils of woodlands.

White Wildflowers

Indian Pipe

Monotropa uniflora

Summer. Plants are 5 to 6 inches tall. Entire plant is waxy-white due to lack of chlorophyll, but will blacken with age. Grows on exposed humus of shady woods.

White Wildflowers

Ladies Tresses
Spiranthes cernua
Summer to fall. Plants are 6 to 12 inches tall with linear, narrow leaves. Its white flowers occur in a spiral arrangement at the top of the stem. Grow in wetlands.

White Wildflowers

May Apple
Podophyllum peltatum
Spring. Plants are 10 to 18 inches tall with one or two shiny green, umbrella-shaped leaves. Plant has single nodding 1.5 inch white flowers. Prefers woodlands.

White Wildflowers

Partridgeberry
Mitchella repens
Spring. Creeping, evergreen plants with opposite, leathery leaves .3 to .75 inch long. Its fragrant white flowers are .5 inch, tiny, paired trumpets. Plant grows in woodlands, preferring acidic soils.

White Wildflowers

Queen Anne's Lace
Daucus carota
Summer. Two to 3 feet tall with a stiff stem, plant has divided, lace-like leaves. Its white flower tops measure up to 5 inches across and also have a lace-like appearance. Plant is common in old fields and waste places.

White Wildflowers

Ramp

Allium tricoccum

Summer. Plants are 8 to 12 inches with gray-green, lance-shaped leaves. Its tight cluster of .25 inch flowers sit atop a 10 inch stem. The root bulb and leaves can be eaten in early spring. It grows in moisture-rich woods.

White Wildflowers

Rattlesnake Orchid
Goodyera pubescens
Summer. Basal flattened rosette of grey-green leaves with white checkerboard veins. Small, white flowers in a dense, terminal cluster on a 6 to 12 inch flower stem. Prefers dry woodlands, often under conifers.

White Wildflowers

Spotted Wintergreen
Chimaphila maculata
Summer. Plants are 3 to 8 inches tall. Each linear, evergreen leaf has a single, white stripe. Its white flowers are .65 inches wide, waxy and cup-shaped, with 4 to 5 petals each. Prefer dry oak or coniferous woodlands.

White Wildflowers

Squirrel Corn
Dicentra canadensis
Spring. Plant measures 6 to 8 inches. It has delicate, dissected leaves and a heart-shaped white flower with semi-fused petals. The plant gets its name from its pea-sized tuberous roots that resemble a corn grain. It is found in moist, rich woods throughout the state.

White Wildflowers

Sweet Clover
Melilotus officinalis
Spring to fall. Plants are 2 to 5 feet tall with small, toothed leaves. It bears numerous, .25 inch, pea-like, white flowers. Is non-native and invasive. Grows along roadsides and in fields.

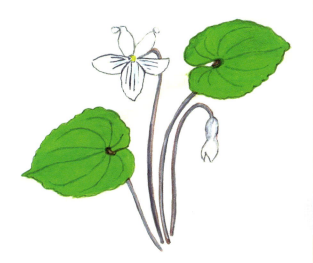

Sweet White Violet

Viola blanda

Spring. Plants are 2 to 4 inches tall. Each of its dark green, shiny leaves rise on a separate stalk. The flowers are .5 inch long, and are held above the leaves. These prefer moist soils.

White Wildflowers

Tall Flat Topped Aster
Aster umbellatus
Summer to fall. Plants grow 2 to 7 feet tall with numerous, alternate, lance-shaped leaves, 2 to 6 inches long. Plant has numerous white ray flower heads with golden centers that are each less than 1 inch across. Appear mostly in mountain areas.

White Wildflowers

Teaberry
Gaultheria procumbens
Spring. Plants are 2 to 6 inches tall with trailing, vine-like shiny evergreen leaves. Flowers are .5 to .75 inch long; tubular flowers dangle from leaf axils. Considered edible wintergreen-flavored berries and leaves. Found under oak or coniferous woods.

White Wildflowers

Turtlehead
Chelone glabra

Summer to fall. Plants are 1 to 3 feet tall. Flowers are in compact cluster up to 2 inches wide. Snapdragon-like flowers resemble open-mouthed turtle heads. Leaves are opposite, lance-shaped, and 3 to 6 inches long. Like wet thickets.

White Wildflowers

Water Hemlock
Cicuta maculata

Spring to summer. Plants are 3 to 6 feet tall, many branched with divided, sharply pointed leaves 1 to 3 inches long. Tiny white flowers are in flattened clusters up to 3 inches at top of plant. Highly poisonous plant! Grows in wet thickets, ditches, and meadows.

White Wildflowers

White Snakeroot
Eupatorium rugosum
Summer to fall. Plants are 1 to 3 feet tall with opposite, serrated leaves. Numerous bright white flowers at the top of stem. Grow in moist woodlands and roadsides.

White Wildflowers

Woodland Aster
Eurybia divaricata
Summer to fall. Plants are 1 to 3 feet tall with zig-zag stems bearing semi-heart shaped, tooth-edged leaves with narrow tips. Flower heads up to 1 inch across at top of stem. Grow on woodland slopes.

Shrubs & Vines

Autumn olive
Elaeagnus umbellata
Shrub grows to 15 feet and is often thorny. The leaves are 2 to 5 inches, green on top and silvery beneath. Bears yellowish, highly fragrant flowers in spring. Also bears a reddish, juicy berry.

Black Elderberry
Sambucus canadensis
Shrub growing to 10 feet tall with weak branches with 5 to 11 lance-shaped leaflets. Its small flowers are white and numerous. The fruit is dark purple and grows in a cluster.

Shrubs & Vines

Blackberry

Rubus spp.
Sprawling, thorny shrubs growing from 5 to 10 feet tall. Angular stems have broad-based prickles and leaves 3 to 8 inches long. The compound leaves grow 3 to 7 palm-like leaflets which are often hairy on underside. The flowers are white in flat clusters; the blackberry fruit is edible.

Shrubs & Vines

Bush Honeysuckles
Lonicera spp.

Three of the more common species that are collectively called bush honeysuckles are Morrow, Tatarian, and Amur honeysuckles. These shrubs grow to 15 feet and are highly invasive in fields and woods. Its leaves are 2 to 3 inches long and opposite. Some are long-tipped while others are egg-shaped. Has hollow twigs. Its flowers are yellowish-white or pinkish in opposite pairs with 4 at a node. The fruit is red, round and juicy. Its foliage is yellowish or brown.

Shrubs & Vines

Common *or* Downy Serviceberry
Amelanchier arborea
This shrub can grow to 20 feet. Its bark is smooth and gray with alternating 2 to 3 inch leaves. The leaves are egg-shaped with toothed margins. Features drooping clusters of white flowers with 5 strap-shaped petals. Its edible berry is red-purple; fall foliage is yellow to reddish-yellow.

Shrubs & Vines

Crab Apple
Malus coronaria

This shrub grows to 20 feet and has spiny branches. Its leaves are 2 to 5 inches long, hairless and rounded at the base. The flowers are showy, pink, and aromatic. The fruit is 1-2 inches wide, green-yellow with a bitter taste. Fall foliage is yellowish.

Shrubs & Vines

Dutchman's Pipevine

Aristolochia macrophylla
A high climbing woody vine with large heart-shaped leaves measuring 4 to 12 inches wide. The flower measures 2 to 3 inches and is colored brown-purple to yellow-green.

Shrubs & Vines

Dwarf (winged) Sumac
Rhus copallinum
Shrub growing to 8 feet tall with shiny leaves 6 to 14 inches long. The leaves are compound, with 11 to 23 leaflets. Its twigs are velvety with raised dots. Clusters of tiny greenish-yellow flowers form red hair-covered berries. The fall foliage is purplish to red or yellow.

Shrubs & Vines

Common Greenbrier
Smilax rotundifolia
Spring to summer. This densetrailing vine grows to 15 feet. Its shiny green tendrils coil around other plant stems. With shiny, green, rounded leaves 2 to 5 inches across, it bears tiny, yellowish-green flowers common in most dry wooded areas.

Shrubs & Vines

Hawthorn
Crataegus spp.
Appearing as a shrub or small tree, the hawthorn is difficult to identify. General characteristics include 1 to 2 inch thorns on branches and trunk. Its small white flowers appear in flat to rounded showy clusters. Bears red or yellow apple-like fruits eaten by wildlife in winter. Its fall foliage is mostly yellow or red.

Shrubs & Vines

Hercules' Club or Devil's Walking Stick

Aralia spinosa

Small tree growing to 20 feet. Its large stems and twigs are covered with sharp spines. Its compound leaves are 2 to 4 inches long with a spiny leaf stalk. The flowers are large, white, flat clusters. Its fruit are black berries. Fall foliage is yellow.

Shrubs & Vines

Ironwood *or* **Muscle Tree**
Carpinus caroliniana
Large shrub grows to 30 feet. Its smooth gray bark has muscle-like ridges. Its leaves are 1 to 5 inches long, alternate and egg-shaped. Its fruit are small nuts in a 3-pointed leafy bract. The fall foliage is reddish-yellow.

Shrubs & Vines

Japanese Barberry
Berberis thunbergii
A compact shrub that grows to six feet. Twigs have yellow inner bark and sharp spines. Leaves are .5 to 1 inch, alternate, wedge-shaped with smooth margins. Small yellow flowers have six petals. Has numerous bright red berries. Fall foliage is red to purple.

Shrubs & Vines

Mountain Laurel
Kalmia latifolia
An evergreen shrub that grows to 10 feet with twisted stems. Leaves are smooth, leathery and 2 to 5 inches. Has numerous white to pink, cup-shaped flowers. Likes dry-acid soils.

Shrubs & Vines

Multiflora Rose
Rosa multiflora

A 10 foot shrub with arching branches covered with sharp, curved spines. Its leaves are compound with 7 to 9 leaflets. Flowers are large, fragrant, white clusters. Bearing a reddish fruit, its fall foliage is yellow.

Shrubs & Vines

Ninebark

Physocarpus opulifolius

A shrub growing to 12 feet on stream banks, its bark grows in thin, shredded layers. Its heart-shaped leaves are 2 to 5 inches long and 3 lobed. Its small, white flowers appear in rounded clusters. It bears small, bladder-like reddish fruit. The fall foliage is reddish-brown.

Shrubs & Vines

Great Laurel *or* **Rhododendron**
Rhododendron maximum
Shrub or small tree growing to 30 feet tall that form dense thickets. Leathery leaves 4 to 8 inches long have rolled edges, especially in winter. The flower is white to pink in large round clusters. Found in rich soil as an understory in ravines and open woodlands. Plant is the West Virginia state flower.

Shrubs & Vines

Poison Ivy

Toxicodendron radicans

Climbing, straggling vine that has compound leaves with 3 leaflets. The fruit is a yellowish clustered berry. Widespread in fields, woodlands, and along stream banks. Contact with any part of the plant can produce allergic reaction causing itching, skin rash, and blistering. Fall foliage is yellow to scarlet.

Shrubs & Vines

Purple Laurel *or* Mountain Rosebay
Rhododendron catawbiense
An evergreen shrub growing to 15 feet, found in southeastern WV, but also planted elsewhere. Leaves are 3 to 7 inches, white on the underside. Grows large purple flowers in showy clusters. Prefers rich soils in ravines and open woodlands. Often found near *Rhododendron maximum*. The fruit is rusty-hairy capsule.

Shrubs & Vines

Redbud
Cercis canadensis
Small tree or shrub growing to 30 feet. Heart-shaped leaves with a smooth margin that are 2 to 6 inches long. The flowers are pink to reddish-purple, growing in showy clusters on stems and branches. Grows best on dry woodlands and roadsides. The fruit is a flat pod. Its fall foliage is yellow.

Smooth *or* Brookside Alder
Alnus serrulata
Shrub growing to 15 feet has dark gray bark. Egg-shaped leaves with sharp-toothed margins are 2 to 5 inches. The male flowers are slender, greenish, and dangling; the female fruit is cone-like and woody. They prefer streambanks and swamps. Fall foliage is green until frost.

Smooth Black Haw
Viburnum prunifolium
This small tree rarely reaches 30 feet. Its barks is thin, divided into reddish-brown scales. Its 1 to 3 inch leaves are dark green above and finely-toothed. Its roots were once used as a nerve tonic. Fall foliage is dull yellow to purplish.

Shrubs & Vines

Spicebush
Lindera benzoin

Shrub growing to 12 feet tall. Egg-shaped leaves are hairless and 2 to 6 inches long. When crushed, leaves have spiced lemony scent. Flowers are small and yellow in early spring and bear bright red fruits. Plant prefers moist forests and fall foliage is yellow.

Shrubs & Vines

Trumpet Creeper
Campsis radicans
Summer to fall. This woody vine grows to 60 feet. Leaves are 4 to 12 inches long. Its orange trumpet-shaped flowers are 2 to 4 inches long. Attracts hummingbirds and bees. Grows on trees and shrubs in full sun.

Shrubs & Vines

Winterberry
Ilex verticillata
Small shrub growing to 15 feet tall. Egg-shaped leaves with coarsely toothed margins are 2 to 3 inches long. Bears bright red fruit. Likes damp areas on edge of wetlands and swamps. Its short-lived fall foliage is yellowish.

Shrubs & Vines

Witch-hazel
Hamamelis virginiana
Shrub or small tree growing to 20 feet. Leaves have wavy margins and a lopsided base; are 2 to 6 inches. Yellow spider-like flowers appear in late autumn. Its fruit is a brownish-yellow 4-parted pod. Fall foliage is yellow.

Shrubs & Vines

Virgin's Bower

Clematis virginiana

Summer. Trailing vine grows over bushes and fence rows by twining leaf stalks. Leaves are 3-parted and often act as tendrils, attaching to support structures so vine can grow upright. Tiny flowers that appear feathery once mature.

Virginia Creeper

Parthenocissus quinquefolia

Summer. A woody vine growing to 40 feet. Has numerous palm-shaped leaves growing to 6 inches across. Grows tiny greenish flowers and bears prominent blue and black berries eaten by over 100 bird species. Widespread in fields, woodlands, and stream banks.

Trees

American Basswood
Tilia americana

Large tree with smooth shallow-fissured gray to gray-brown bark and stout twigs. Four to 6 inch leaves are dark green on top and pale on underside with tufts of brown hairs on veins. Inner bark makes excellent rope. Fall foliage is yellow to brown.

American Beech
Fagus grandifolia
A large tree with tight-fitting, smooth, bluish-gray bark. The 3 to 5 inch, sharply-toothed leaves are dull, greenish-blue on top. Fruits highly prized by wildlife. Its fall foliage is yellow to brown, and remains on twigs through spring.

Trees

American Chestnut
Castanea dentata
Chestnut blight reduced this former tall tree to 20 to 30 foot root suckers. Its bark is orange-brown to dark gray. Leaves are 4 to 8 inches and alternate with a long, sharp tip. Leaf edge has large teeth with a bristle. Fruit is a 2 to 3 inch bur of sharp spines enclosing 1 to 3 brown nuts. Fall foliage is yellow.

American Elm
Ulmus americana
A large tree with a V-shaped crown and light brown to gray bark. Leave are alternate and serrated. Fruit is an oval samara, less than 1 inch. Grows in bottomlands and along riverbanks.

American Holly

Ilex opaca

Small evergreen tree growing to forty feet with smooth gray bark. Leaves are 2 to 4 inches long with sharp spines on leaf margins. A symbol of Christmas, the tree bears red, and occasionally yellow, berries.

Bigtooth Aspen
Populus grandidentata
A medium-sized tree with 3 to 7 inch dark green leaves with a whitish-wooly underside. The leaf stem is perpendicular to main branch. Bark is yellowish-green and gray on young trees. Turns gray and knobby on older trees. Fall foliage is yellow.

Black Cherry

Prunus serotina

A large tree with rounded crown, its inner bark and twigs have a bitter almond aroma and are toxic. Leaves are 2 to 5 inches. Bark is broken into numerous dark patchy scales and is dark brown to black on mature trees. Fall foliage is yellow to red.

Black Gum
Nyssa sylvatica
A large tree with egg-shaped, hairless, shiny, thick, leathery leaves 3 to 6 inches long. Twigs have a chambered pith and fruit is a blue berry. Bark on young trees is gray and smooth; on older trees is gray, blocky and has deep grooves. Fall foliage is yellow to scarlet.

Trees

Black Locust
Robinia pseudo-acacia
Medium-sized tree with 8 to 14 inch compound leaves and 1 to 2 inch leaflets. Branches have paired thorns. Bark is dark brown with criss-crossed furrows. Fall foliage is yellow.

Black Walnut
Juglans nigra

A wide-branching medium to large tree. Bark is dark with thick, blocky patches. Has 12 to 18 inch compound leaves with 7 to 17 leaflets. When crushed, leaves have spicy scent. Pith of twigs is chambered. Fruit is a large round nut. Fall foliage is yellowish.

Trees

Black Willow
Salix nigra
Medium sized tree with a main trunk that forks. Bark is grayish-brown and shaggy with broad ridges. Leaves are 3 to 6 inches long. Trunk tends to lean over streams. Fall foliage is dull yellow.

Box Elder

Acer negundo

Small to medium-sized tree in the maple family. Bark is green-gray on young trees with tight, narrow ridges. Twigs are bright green with a whitish coating. Six to 10 inch compound leaves are pale yellow green. Fall foliage is yellow.

Bradford Pear
Pyrus calleryana
A small ornamental and highly invasive tree, growing to 40 feet. Leaves are 2 to 3 inches, alternate, leathery, dark-green and shiny. In spring has large, showy, white clusters of flowers before leaves. Bears small round brown fruit. Its fall foliage is crimson to wine-red.

Chestnut Oak
Quercus prinus

This large tree has a full, open crown. Its grayish bark with shallow furrows has prominent vertical ridges; older trees are more deeply furrowed. Four to 8 inch leaves are thick and leathery; yellowish-green on top and downy below. Fall foliage is yellow to brown.

Trees

Cucumber Magnolia
Magnolia acuminata
Medium-sized tree with a pyramidal shape and dark brown, furrowed bark. Its 6 to 10 inch leaves are gray-green above and fuzzy below. Has long, silvery buds when dormant. Fall foliage is bright yellow.

Eastern Hemlock

Tsuga canadensis

Large tree with cinnamon-brown bark has purplish inner bark. Its needles are .5 to .75 inches long, flat with a round tip and 2 white lines beneath. Has a .5 to .75 inch egg-shaped cone at end of branches. Prefers ravines and swamps.

Eastern Red Cedar
Juniperus virginiana
A small evergreen tree with reddish brown bark that peels in long strips. Its needles resemble scales or sharp awls; its twigs are often 4-angled. Fruit is a cone that looks like a dark blue berry with a white coating. Prefers old fields, rocky outcrops, limestone or high pH soils.

Flowering Dogwood
Cornus florida
A small tree growing to 30 feet. Has an opposite branching pattern and 4-5 inch oval-shaped leaves. New stems are purplish in color; bark is grayish brown with a blocky appearance. Species is considered a valuable ornamental for its showy white flowers with 4 petal-like bracts; their complete structure measures 3 to 4 inches. Fruit is a small bright red berry.

Honey Locust
Gleditsia tricanthos

A medium-sized tree with dark gray, deeply furrowed bark with flattened, narrow ridges. Has 3 to 4 inch long branched thorns on trunk and branches. Leaves grow up to 15 inches, are dark, shiny green above and yellow-green below. Fall foliage is bright yellow.

Norway Spruce
Picea abies
Introduced from northern Europe, this large evergreen has a rounded crown. Young trees have a reddish or coppery bark, which grows purplish on older trees. Its needles are dark green, 4-sided, sharply pointed, and .5 to .75 inch. The limbs sweep upward with dangling branchlets beneath. Twigs are hairless. The cones are 4 to 6 inches and are shed each year.

Trees

Pawpaw
Asimina triloba
This small to medium-sized tree has thin, dark brown bark with warty blotches that turn gray and mottled. Its smooth, light green leaves are 10 to 14 inches long, widest near the tip. Has prominent red, hairy buds and edible fruit. Fall foliage is deep buttercup yellow.

Trees

Persimmon
Diospyros virginiana
A fifty-foot tree with dark grayish-brown bark broken up into blocks. Leaves are oval-shaped and 4 inches long. Round orange-colored berry has diameter of 1.5 inches. Tree grows in old fields and along roadsides. Fall foliage is orange or yellow.

Pignut Hickory
Carya glabra
A large tree with tight, narrowly-ridged gray bark forming diamond-shaped patterns. Leaves are dark yellow-green above with tufts of hair on underside. Bears pear-shaped fruits. Fall foliage is yellow.

Pin Oak
Quercus palustris
A large tree with firm, thin, tight, gray bark broken into shallow fissures and broad ridges. Its major limbs angle downward and have drooping, slender twigs. The 3 to 6 inch leaves are shiny green on top. Fall foliage is scarlet red.

Trees

Red Maple

Acer rubrum

A large tree with a narrow top. Bark is thin, tight, and light gray. Leaves are 3 to 4 inches, light-green above and silvery below, with red stalks. Buds are red; emerging leaves are red; fruits are reddish and wing-like. Fall foliage is yellow to red.

Red Oak
Quercus rubra
Large tree with a rounded crown. Has dark gray-brown furrowed bark with narrow, shiny, flat, vertical ridges. Leaves are 5 to 9 inches, thin, dark green above and bristle-tipped. Its fruit is an acorn. Fall foliage turns red then chocolate brown.

River Birch
Betula nigra
Grows to 70 feet with salmon pink bark on young growth, turning brown at maturity. Leaves are 3 to 4 inches and deeply-toothed. The fruit resembles a small cone. Tree is found along stream banks.

Trees

Sassafras
Sassafras albidum

A small, often clustered tree. Its bark is reddish-brown with narrow furrows. Twigs and leaves are both strongly aromatic. Leaves are 4 to 6 inches, shiny yellow-green above, occur in 3 shapes. Fall foliage is red to gold.

Trees

Scotch Pine
Pinus sylvestris
This medium-sized evergreen was introduced from Europe and is frequently planted; also spreads from seed. Bark is orangish on upper stems. Needles are 2 per bundle, 2 to 3 inches and twisted. Its cone is 1 to 2 inches, shed each year. Scales have no sharp prickle.

Shagbark Hickory
Carya ovata

A large tree with narrow, conical crown. Its dark gray bark appears peeled into foot-long, upward-curling shreds. Leaves are 8 to 14 inches with 5 to 7 leaflets; dark yellow-green above. Tasty nut is 1.5 inch across, surrounded by smooth husk. Fall foliage is golden yellow.

Trees

Slippery Elm
Ulmus rubra
This medium-sized tree is vase-shaped with a flat crown. Its bark is in flat plates with a dark brown inner color. The leaves alternate, are 4 to 8 inches, rough above and hairy below with a lopsided base. Twigs are rough and hairy; buds are red and hairy; the inner bark is slimy. Oval-shaped samara .5 inch across. Fall foliage is yellow.

Sourwood

Oxydendrum arboreum

A small tree that often leans, it has gray, blocky bark. The leaves are alternate and have a sour taste. Leaves are 4 to 7 inches; leaf margin has very small teeth. Twigs are green or red. Flowers are white in long, showy clusters. Tree often found west of the higher mountains. Fall foliage is red or purple.

Trees

Striped Maple

Acer pensylvanicum

This small tree or shrub is common at elevations above 2,500 feet. The bark on young stems is green with vertical white stripes. Flowers are yellow, bell-shaped and hang in clusters. Leaves 5 to 9 inches, are opposite with 3 large lobes that resemble a goosefoot. Fall foliage is yellow.

Trees

Sugar *or* **Hard Maple**
Acer saccharum

State tree of West Virginia. This large tree is widespread, but thrives in ravines and rich moist upland forests. In fields or yards it is shorter with a round crown. Wood is excellent for furniture, gym floors and bowling lanes. The bark is gray and smooth or bumpy when young and scaly when mature. 4 to 7 inch leaves are opposite with palm-like veins, 5 lobes with U-shaped notches and long tips. The seed is a 2-winged samara. Fall foliage is red or yellow.

Sweet *or* Black Birch
Betula lenta
A medium-sized tree with bark in a dark brown, horizontal pattern. Prefers rich ravines, woodlands, and upland forests. The leaves alternate, are 3 to 5 inches, and often in pairs on stubby twigs. The leaf margins have small, sharp teeth. The twigs have a strong, wintergreen or teaberry taste and smell. Tree grows along roadsides, in disturbed areas and open forests. Fall foliage is yellow.

Sweetgum

Liquidambar styraciflua

This large to medium tree has alternate, star-shaped leaves 3 to 6 inches long with 5 to 7 lobes and fine teeth on margin. The fruits are round with horn-tipped projections on long dangling stems. Are common in floodplains of the New and lower Ohio Rivers, and are also often planted. Found in river bottomlands along major streams. Fall foliage is yellow, red or purple.

Trees

Sycamore
Platanus occidentalis
The bark of these very large trees flakes off to reveal white, green or yellow underbark. The leaves alternate, are 4 to 8 inches long with 3 to 5 lobes and several large teeth. The leafstalk hides the bud in its base. The fruit is a 1 inch round ball on a dangling stem. Common in floodplains and stream banks. Fall foliage is yellow or brown.

Tree-of-heaven
Ailanthus altissima

Large to medium tree with gray bark. Leaves are compound, alternate, 2 to 3 feet long with 11 to 41 leaflets with 2 to 3 small teeth at the base. The crushed leaves and twigs have an offensive odor. Each seed is in the center of a twisted wing. The twig is large and yellow brown. This is an alien, invasive tree in cities and on roadsides that spreads from root suckers and seeds. The leaves are green until killed by frost.

Trees

Tuliptree *or* Yellow Poplar
Liriodendron tulipifera

A large tree with a straight trunk; smooth gray bark seen on young saplings; whitish-gray bark with deep grooves on older trees. Leaves alternate, are 3 to 7 inches with smooth margins, 4 lobes, and a flat or slight V tip. The flower is tulip-like with yellow petals and orange base. The fruit is a pointed cone of samaras. The buds are green or purple. Found in rich woods or old fields. Fall foliage is yellow.

Virginia Pine
Pinus virginiana
This small to medium evergreen is short-lived, usually to sixty years. Needles are 2 per bundle, twisted, 2 to 3 inches long. The twigs are yellow, whitish or purple. The cones are egg-shaped, 2 to 3 inches with very sharp prickles on scales which persist on tree for years. Often found on old fields and roadsides.

White Ash
Fraxinus americana

This large tree's bark is light gray and blocky. The leaves are compound, opposite, 8 to 12 inches long with 5 to 9 leaflets, smooth margins and a soft hairy underside. The twigs are stout with rounded buds. The fruit is a cluster of winged samaras with seed in base. Usually found in rich woods, old fields, and roadsides. Fall foliage is yellow to purple.

White Oak
Quercus alba

Large tree with a broad crown. Bark is gray to whitish and scaly. Leaves alternate, 4 to 9 inches with 5 to 11 rounded lobes; hairless and whitened beneath, clustered at tip of twigs. Its acorn is 1 inch long in shallow knobby cup. Found on dry hillsides. Fall foliage is red, brown, yellowish or purple.

White Pine
Pinus strobus

A large, very tall evergreen common in eastern West Virginia and patchy in western West Virginia; is planted throughout. Limbs that sweep upward grow in whorls of 1 per year. Needles are 2 to 5 inches, 5 per bundle, flexible, whitish green in color, persist for 2 to 3 years before shedding. The cone is 4 to 10 inches long, resinous. Likes old fields, well-drained woodlands, and is often planted as an ornamental.

Yellow Buckeye

Aesculus octandra or flava

This medium to large-sized tree grows in rich woods and floodplains. It has smooth gray bark or broad plates on older trees. Leaves are opposite with 5 palm-like leaflets, 4 to 15 inches. Twigs are stout with reddish-brown buds. Its spongy husk hold 1 to 3 poisonous nuts. The seed is brown with a light brown spot (called eye of buck deer). Foliage often turns yellow or red in late summer.

Index

Acer negundo 147
Acer pensylvanicum 168
Acer rubrum 160
Acer saccharum 169
Aesculus octandra or *flava* 179
Ailanthus altissima 173
Alder, Brookside 128
Alder, Smooth 128
Alexander's, Golden 12
Alliaria petiolata 89
Allium tricoccum 96
Alnus serrulata 128
Amelanchier arborea 112
American Basswood 136
American Beech 137
American Chestnut 138
American Elm 139
American Holly 140
Amur Honeysuckle 111
Apple, Crab 113
Apple, May 93
Aquilegia canadensis 31
Aralia spinosa 118
Arbutus, Trailing 75
Arisaema triphyllum 35
Aristolochia macrophylla 114
Arrowhead, Common 82
Asarum canadense 37
Asclepias syriaca 61
Asclepias tuberosa 24
Ash, White 176

Asimina triloba 156
Aspen, Bigtooth 141
Aster, New England 52
Aster, Tall Flat Topped 102
Aster, Woodland 107
Aster umbellatus 102
Aureolaria laevigata 11
Autumn Olive 108
Barberry, Japanese 120
Basswood, American 136
Beard Tongue 59
Bee Balm 29
Beech, American 137
Beggar-tick, Common 7
Bellflower, Tall 55
Bellwort 1
Berberis thunbergii 120
Bergamot, Wild 44
Betula lenta 170
Betula nigra 162
Bidens vulgata 7
Bigtooth Aspen 141
Birch, Black 170
Birch, River 162
Birch, Sweet 170
Birdsfoot Trefoil 2
Black Birch 170
Black Cherry 142
Black Cohosh 77
Black Elderberry 109
Black Gum 143
Black Locust 144
Black Walnut 145

Black Willow 146
Blackberry 110
Black-eyed Susan 3
Bleeding Heart, Wild 76
Bloodroot 78
Blue Cohosh 34
Blue Vervain 38
Bluebells 40
Blue-eyed Grass 39
Bluets 41
Boneset 79
Bouncing Bet 60
Bower, Virgin's 134
Box Elder 147
Bradford Pear 148
Breeches, Dutchman's 87
Brookside Alder 128
Buckeye, Yellow 179
Bugleweed 80
Bugloss, Viper 56
Bush Honeysuckle 111
Butter & Eggs 4
Butterfly Milkweed 24
Cabbage, Skunk 36
Campanula americana 55
Campsis radicans 131
Canada Goldenrod 5
Canada Violet 81
Cardamine concapenata 85
Cardinal Flower 30
Carpinus caroliniana 119
Carya glabra 158
Carya ovata 165

Castanea dentate 138
Caullophylum thalictroides 34
Cedar, Eastern Red 152
Cercis canadensis 127
Chelone glabra 104
Cherry, Black 142
Chestnut Oak 149
Chestnut, American 138
Chickory 42
Chickweed, Common 83
Chicorum intybus 42
Chimaphila maculata 98
Cicuta maculata 105
Cimcifuga racemosa 77
Cinquefoil, Common 8
Cirsium vulgare 66
Claytonia virginica 84
Clematis virginiana 134
Clover, Sweet 100
Cohosh, Black 77
Cohosh, Blue 34
Colt's Foot 6
Columbine 31
Common Arrowhead 82
Common Beggar-ticks 7
Common Chickweed 83
Common Cinquefoil 8
Common Greenbrier 116
Common Milkweed 61
Common Monkey Flower 43
Common Mullein 9
Common Serviceberry 112
Common Spring Beauty 84

181

Common St. Johnswort 17
Corn, Squirrel 99
Cornus florida 153
Coronilla varia 63
Crab Apple 113
Crataegus spp. 117
Creeper, Trumpet 131
Creeper, Virginia 135
Creeping Phlox 62
Crown Vetch 63
Cucumber Magnolia 150
Cut-leaved Toothwort 85
Daisy Fleabane 86
Dame's Rocket 64
Daucus carota 95
Day Lily 25
Delphinium tricorne 46
Deptford Pink 65
Devil's Walking Stick 118
Dianthus armeria 65
Dicentra canadensis 99
Dicentra cucullaria 87
Dicentra eximia 76
Diospyros virginiana 157
Dogwood, Flowering 153
Downy Serviceberry 112
Duck Potato 82
Dutchman's Breeches 87
Dutchman's Pipevine 114
Dwarf (winged) Sumac 115
Dwarf Crested Iris 45
Dwarf Larkspur 46
Eastern Hemlock 151

Eastern Red Cedar 152
Echium vulgare 56
Elaeagnus umbellata 108
Elderberry, Black 109
Elm, American 139
Elm, Slippery 166
Epigaea repens 75
Epilobium angustifolium 67
Erigeron annuus 86
Erythronium americanum 20
Eupatorium coelestinum 51
Eupatorium fistulosum 70
Eupatorium perfoliatum 79
Eupatorium rugosum 106
Eurybia divaricata 107
Evening Primrose 10
Fagus grandifolia 137
Field Hawkweed 26
Field Thistle 66
Fire Pink 32
Fireweed 67
Flowering Dogwood 153
Foam Flower 88
Foxglove, Smooth 11
Fraxinus americana 176
Garlic Mustard 89
Gaultheria procumbens 103
Geranium maculatum 58
Geranium, Wild 58
Ginger, Wild 37
Glechoma hederacea 48
Gleditsia triacnathos 154
Golden Alexander's 12

Goldenrod, Canada 5
Goldenrod, Wreath 22
Goodyera pubescens 97
Grass, Blue-eyed 39
Great Laurel 124
Great Lobelia 47
Great White Trillium 90
Greenbrier, Common 116
Ground Ivy 48
Gum, Black 143
Hamamelis virginiana 133
Hard Maple 169
Haw, Smooth Black 129
Hawkweed, Field 26
Hawthorn 117
Heal-all 49
Heaven, Tree-of 173
Helianthus decapetalus 19
Helianthus divaricatus 21
Hemerocalus fulva 25
Hemlock, Eastern 151
Hemlock, Water 105
Hepatica 68
Hepatica spp. 68
Hercules' Club 118
Hesparis matrinalis 64
Hibiscus moscheutos 74
Hickory, Pignut 158
Hickory, Shagbark 165
Hieracium caespitosum 26
Hieracium venosum 16
Holly, American 140
Honey Locust 154

Honeysuckle, Bush 111
Houstonia spp. 41
Hypericum perforatum 17
Ilex opaca 140
Ilex verticillata 132
Impatiens capensis 27
Impatiens pallida 15
Indian Pipe 91
Iris, Dwarf Crested 45
Iris, Yellow Flag 23
Iris cristata 45
Iris pseudoacaris 23
Ironweed 69
Ironwood 119
Ivy, Ground 48
Ivy, Poison 125
Jack-in-the-Pulpit 35
Japanese Barberry 120
Joe Pye Weed 70
Juglans nigra 145
Juniperus virginiana 152
Kalmia latifolia 121
Lace, Queen Anne's 95
Ladies Tresses 92
Larkspur, Dwarf 46
Laurel, Great 124
Laurel, Mountain 121
Laurel, Purple 126
Lilium superbum 28
Lily, Day 25
Lily, Trout 20
Lily, Turk's Cap 28
Linaria vulgaris 4

183

Lindera benzoin 130
Liquidambar styraciflua 171
Liriodendron tulipifera 174
Lobelia, Great 47
Lobelia cardinalis 30
Lobelia siphilitica 47
Locust, Black 144
Locust, Honey 154
Lonicera spp. 111
Lotus corniculatus 2
Lousewort 13
Lycopis virginicus 80
Mad-dog Skullcap 50
Magnolia, Cucumber 150
Magnolia acuminata 150
Malus coronaria 113
Maple, Hard 169
Maple, Red 160
Maple, Striped 168
Maple, Sugar 169
May Apple 93
Melilotus officinalis 100
Mertensia virginica 40
Milkweed, Butterfly 24
Milkweed, Common 61
Mimulus ringens 43
Mistflower 51
Mitchella repens 94
Monarda didyma 29
Monarda fistulosa 44
Monkey, Common Flower 43
Monotropa uniflora 91
Morrow's Honeysuckle 111

Moth Mullein 14
Mountain Laurel 121
Mountain Rosebay 126
Mullein, Common 9
Mullein, Moth 14
Multiflora Rose 122
Muscle Tree 119
Mustard, Garlic 89
New England Aster 52
Ninebark 123
Norway Spruce 155
Nyssa sylvatica 143
Oak, Chestnut 149
Oak, Pin 159
Oak, Red 161
Oak, White 177
Oenothera biennis 10
Olive, Autumn 108
Orchid, Rattlesnake 97
Oxydendrum arboreum 167
Pale Touch-me-not 15
Parthenocissus quinquefolia 135
Partridgeberry 94
Pasture Rose 71
Pawpaw 156
Pear, Bradford 148
Pedicularis canadensis 13
Penstemon spp. 59
Periwinkle 53
Persimmon 157
Phlox, Creeping 62
Phlox, Wild Blue 57

Phlox divaricata 57
Phlox stolonifera 62
Physocarpus opulifolius 123
Picea abies 155
Pignut Hickory 158
Pin Oak 159
Pine, Scotch 164
Pine, Virginia 175
Pine, White 178
Pink, Deptford 65
Pink, Fire 32
Pink, Rose 72
Pinus strobus 178
Pinus sylvestris 164
Pinus virginiana 175
Pipevine, Dutchman's 114
Platanus occidentalis 172
Podophyllum peltatum 93
Poison Ivy 125
Polygala sanguinicea 73
Poplar, Yellow 174
Populus grandidentata 141
Potentilla simplex 8
Primrose, Evening 10
Prunella vulgaris 49
Prunus serotina 142
Purple Laurel 126
Pyrus calleryana 148
Queen Anne's Lace 95
Quercus alba 177
Quercus palustris 159
Quercus prinus 149
Quercus rubra 161

Ramp 96
Rattlesnake Orchid 97
Rattlesnake Weed 16
Red Maple 160
Red Oak 161
Redbud 127
Rhododendron 124
Rhododendron catawbiense 126
Rhododendron maximum 124
Rhus copallinum 115
River Birch 162
Robinia pseudo-acacia 144
Rocket, Dame's 64
Rosa caroliniana 71
Rosa multiflora 122
Rose Pink 72
Rose Polygala 73
Rose, Multiflora 122
Rose, Pasture 71
Rose, Swamp Mallow 74
Rosebay, Mountain 126
Rubus spp. 110
Rudbeckia hirta 3
Sabatia angularis 72
Saggitaria latifolia 82
Salix nigra 146
Sambucus canadensis 109
Sanguinaria canadensis 78
Saponaria officinalis 60
Sassafras 163
Sassafras albidum 163
Scotch Pine 164
Scutellaria lateriflora 50

185

Serviceberry, Common 112
Serviceberry, Downy 112
Shagbark Hickory 165
Silene virginica 32
Sisyrinchium angustifolium 39
Skullcap, Mad-dog 50
Skunk Cabbage 36
Slippery Elm 166
Smilax rotundifolia 116
Smooth Alder 128
Smooth Black Haw 129
Smooth Foxglove 11
Snakeroot, White 106
Solidago caesia 22
Solidago canadensis 5
Sourwood 167
Spicebush 130
Spiderwort 54
Spiranthes cernua 92
Spotted Touch-me-not 27
Spotted Wintergreen 98
Spring Beauty, Common 84
Spruce, Norway 155
Squirrel Corn 99
St. Johnswort, Common 17
Stellaria media 83
Striped Maple 168
Sugar Maple 169
Sumac, Dwarf Winged 115
Sunflower, Thin Leaved 19
Sunflower, Woodland 21
Swamp Rose Mallow 74
Sweet Birch 170

Sweet Clover 100
Sweet White Violet 101
Sweetgum 171
Sycamore 172
Symphyotrichum novae-angliae 52
Symplocarpus foetidus 36
Tall Bellflower 55
Tall Flat Topped Aster 102
Tatarian Honeysuckle 111
Teaberry 103
Thin Leaved Sunflower 19
Thistle, Field 66
Tiarella cordifollia 88
Tilia americana 136
Toothwort, Cut-leaved 85
Touch-me-not, Pale 15
Touch-me-not, Spotted 27
Toxicodendron radicans 125
Tradescantia spp. 54
Trailing Arbutus 75
Tree-of-Heaven 173
Tresses, Ladies 92
Trillium grandiflorum 90
Trillium, Great White 90
Trillium erectum 33
Trout Lily 20
Trumpet Creeper 131
Tsuga canadensis 151
Tuliptree 174
Turk's Cap Lily 28
Turtlehead 104
Tussilago farfara 6

Ulmus americana 139
Ulmus rubra 166
Uvularia spp. 1
Verbascum blattaria 14
Verbascum thapsus 9
Verbena hastata 38
Vernonia noveboracensis 69
Vervain, Blue 38
Vetch, Crown 63
Viburnum prunifolium 129
Vinca minor 53
Viola blanda 101
Viola canadensis 81
Viola pubescens 18
Violet, Canada 81
Violet, Sweet White 101
Violet, Yellow Woodland 18
Vipers Bugloss 56
Virgin's Bower 134
Virginia Creeper 135
Virginia Pine 175
Wake Robin 33
Walking Stick, Devil's 118
Walnut, Black 145
Water Hemlock 105
Weed, Joe Pye 70
Weed, Rattlesnake 16
White Ash 176
White Oak 177
White Pine 178
White Snakeroot 106
Wild Bergamot 44
Wild Bleeding Heart 76
Wild Blue Phlox 57
Wild Geranium 58
Wild Ginger 37
Willow, Black 146
Winterberry 132
Wintergreen, Spotted 98
Witch-hazel 133
Woodland Aster 107
Woodland Sunflower 21
Wreath Goldenrod 22
Yellow Buckeye 179
Yellow Flag Iris 23
Yellow Poplar 174
Yellow Woodland Violet 18
Zizia aptera 12

187